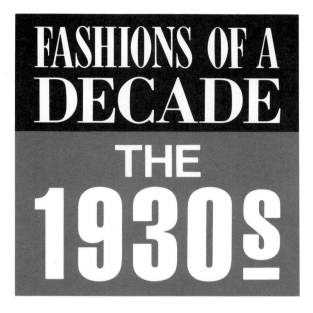

FASHIONS OF A DECADE
THE
1930s

FASHIONS OF A DECADE
THE 1930s

Maria Costantino

**Series Editors: Valerie Cumming and
Elane Feldman
Original Illustrations by Robert Price**

Facts On File
New York • Oxford

Contents

Facts On File, Inc.
460 Park Avenue South
New York NY 10016

Facts On File books are available at special discounts when purchased in bulk quantities for businesses, associations, institutions or sales promotions. Please call our Special Sales Department in New York at 212/683–2244 (dial 800/322-8755 except in NY, AK or HI).

Text design by David Stanley
Jacket design by David Stanley
Composition by Latimer Trend
Manufactured by Bookbuilders Ltd
Printed in Hong Kong

10 9 8 7 6 5 4 3 2 1

This book is printed on acid-free paper.

Library of Congress Cataloging-in-Publication Data
Costantino, Maria.
    Fashions of a decade. The 1930s/Maria Costantino.
    P.   cm.
    Includes bibliographical references and index.
        Summary: Chronicles trends in 1930s styles such as lower hemlines and broader shoulders; the introduction of synthetic fabrics; and new views of fitness, health, and personal beauty.
    ISBN 0–8160–2466–9
    1. Costume—History—20th century—Juvenile literature.
    2. Fashion—History—20th century—Juvenile literature.
    [1. Costume—History—20th century. 2. Fashion—History—20th century. [I. Title.
    GT596.C67   1992
    391'.009 043—dc20

THE 30S

The thirties were a decade that opened in depression and ended in war. Throughout the 1920s economies worldwide had been booming, bringing prosperity to thousands of ordinary people who gambled their spare cash on stocks and shares. But in 1929 the economy of the Western world sank deep into a period of depression.

The downward spiral began with an excess of agricultural products, which led to falling prices and, in order to control the decline, produce was kept off the markets. The fall in agricultural prices meant that the farming population faced a reduced income. When agricultural prices began to fall, in America at least, investors in industry remained optimistic and the price of

stocks was still rising in early 1929. With this investment in industry, manufacturers were able to increase their output: in 1929 the automobile industry produced around five-and-a-half million cars. But the industrialists soon began to realize that the market would become saturated and they would have to check production. Doubts turned to fears, which in turn grew into panic, as people raced to withdraw their investments. On October 24, 1929, 13 million shares were sold on Wall Street, the financial heart of America. One company after another crashed as its credit failed and, by the end of the month, American investors had lost some $40 billion.

Unemployment rose while purchasing power collapsed. Large businesses collapsed, often taking smaller ones with them. Thousands of small investors lost everything and, in the industrialized towns and cities, unemployed workers joined breadlines. By 1932 three million were out of work in Britain, six million in Germany and 14 million in America.

Generally then, when we think of the 1930s, our minds conjure up images of despair: mass unemployment and breadlines, the rise of fascism and the drift toward World War II. With these images firmly planted in our minds, it is easy to forget that fashion, beauty and glamour were still important aspects of everyday life for many people.

Tightening the Belt

If fashion had merely been a luxury, during the 1930s, the industry would have totally collapsed. Instead, it was to respond to all the economic and social changes of the decade and would be swayed by the opposing influences of the economic climate and the impact of Hollywood-style luxury.

As the rich were tightening their belts, spending less and making economies where they could, designers responded by cutting their prices, producing new lines of ready-to-wear clothes to make up for the shortfall in orders for couture garments, and by producing more practical clothes made of economical and washable fabrics. In 1931, Gabrielle "Coco" Chanel showed a collection of evening dresses that helped to promote

Models from—
LUCIEN LELONG

No paper patterns can be supplied of the French models on this page.

Dinner Frocks have Short Sleeves

It is new, and it is welcome—the fashion for short sleeves in dinner frocks. It allows the dress to be worn so much more often than a very formal design, and it is always delightful in effect. The dress above is in the new Andalusian blue satin trimmed with "twists" of palest pink georgette. On the right is a distinguished dress with a draped bodice of off-white crêpe romain, and a skirt of brown crêpe-de-Chine, and another lovely frock of green satin with attractive bow-trimmed sleeves.

Transitional. 1932 dinner frocks from the House of Lelong. The longer length and slimmer cut are countered by the crisscross necklines, which still retain a feel of the previous decade.

The Material Sets the Hour

No paper patterns can be obtained of these Paris models.

For the morning a dress of Bordeaux red Madiana. The fall of the collar on this neat dress, the bow, and the looped basque effect are all new and interesting. The shoulders are cut to look broad, and the waist is well defined. For the afternoon there is the coat and dress of crêpe marocain in beige and nigger brown. In this you see how cleverly contrast can be used to give an outline which is slender. The dark bands down the arms and on the front of the coat give a deceptive outline. For the evening. Lelong makes this frock of sea blue lace. It is the kind of dress that looks as charming at an informal dinner as in a ballroom, since its uncommon puff sleeves are smart enough for any gathering, yet are also the reason for labelling the dress "informal."

Models — LELONG

45

E

cotton as a fashion fabric and by 1932, she had also cut nearly 50 percent off her prices.

There were also new fabrics for designers to work with: what were then called artificial silks like rayon were now stronger and better, and in 1939 the production of nylon began in the United States. Nylon was stronger and more elastic than previous artificial silks. In addition to a whole host of pre-shrunk, or Sanforized, fabrics

there were uncrushable fabrics like the one called Zingale and glass fabrics such as one known as Rhodophane, which Elsa Schiaparelli used to sensational effect.

For women who could afford them, the fashions of the early thirties were stylish and elegant. The longer and more flowing lines that the Paris-based couturiers had shown in their collections in the autumn of 1929 were to become established in 1930. But the increas-

More outfits from Lucien Lelong, for (right to left) morning, afternoon and evening. All three designs employ broad shoulders and narrow waists to define their overall shape, in addition to contrasting effects of texture and color in their use of fabrics.

ingly difficult economic situation meant that many women simply could not afford the luxury of new clothes. In an effort to bring up-to-date their existing shorter length skirts, many women resorted to adding lengthening bands of contrasting fabric or even fur to their hems. Material was often added to collars and sleeves to give the impression that their outfit had been designed that way and was not simply an emergency measure.

Within a year the new lines for fashion had been established and, as if they were mirroring the economic slump, hemlines dropped. Longer and narrower skirts that gradually flared out fell to the bottom of the calf. Longer hair was waved lower on to the nape of the neck. Hats featured skull caps with draped folds of fabric attached to the back or sides, or brims that obscured one eye. Sleeves were now full from the elbow to the wrist, where they dropped on to cuffs or were loosely tied.

Also reflecting the subdued mood of the early thirties were colors: black, navy and gray were popular for city wear; browns and greens were popular for autumn outfits. For afternoon wear and evening dresses, black or pastel shades of peach, pink, green and blue were the most fashionable.

Dust bowl refugees head for Los Angeles, 1937. From 1934 through the late 1930s the U.S. prairie states were hit with annual dust storms. From December to May, huge black clouds of soil were blown off farmland that had been overplanted and overgrazed by livestock. Many who lived in those states were left with nothing and so headed west to California, which had come to be considered a promised land with jobs for all.

New Deal

On a cold, windy day, March 4, 1933, Franklin Delano Roosevelt took the presidential oath and addressed America with the words: "This great nation will endure as it has endured, will revive and will prosper." Roosevelt seemed to promise, as his popular campaign song indicated, "Happy Days Are Here Again."

The plan to revive the flagging American economy and national spirit was called the New Deal, and the president's first act was to rescue the banks, many of which had gone bankrupt and closed. In the first of his famous Fireside Chats on the radio, FDR announced that the banks would reopen the next day. All over America people listened to the president, and many believed in his ability to lead them out of the depression. The next day, bank deposits exceeded withdrawals.

To continue the work of cheering everyone up, Roosevelt announced that it was a good time for a beer and pressed for the repeal of the

Eighteenth Amendment, which had prohibited the manufacture and sale of intoxicating liquors in the USA since 1920.

But FDR did not lose sight of many other important issues. The New Deal program of reforms instituted help for mortgaged farmers and tennants by taking steps to prevent their mortgage holders and landlords from foreclosing and so leaving them homeless. The national government also went to the rescue of the jobless with a federal payroll of $500 million used to put the unemployed back to work. On Muscle Shoals in Tennessee, the river was used to generate cheap electrical power for the people of the Tennessee Valley.

The New Deal program had something for everyone – farmers, workers, even writers and artists – with a government-sponsored program of public art and writing projects – and reflected Roosevelt's hope that he could lead a united country along the road to recovery.

"Whether she speaks English, French, Spanish, Italian or Yankee Americanese . . . her gown proclaims in the very shade and texture of its fabric the worldwide preference for Stehli Silk" reads the ad text. The desirable fabric of the decade, nothing would cut and drape like silk, in the bias cuts and folds of thirties couture.

Pleats from the knees, cloche hats, contrasting weaves; late thirties daywear by Captain Edward Molyneux.

Moving with the Movies

Although designers still continued to create lavish gowns for royalty and the rich, they were also taking into account the requirements of the working lives that more and more ordinary women were leading. The changed role that women were playing in society and the gradual weakening of clearly defined social distinctions that had begun at the beginning of the century meant that many more people were sharing similar life-styles. During the day women might be working in offices or in light industry, while their evenings were spent dancing or at the theater or cinema.

If radio was the miracle of the twenties, the miracle of the thirties was the talking picture. Sound movies had arrived in 1927, but it was in the thirties that they were truly ''all talking, all singing, all dancing'' spectaculars. While the rich and royal may still have looked to Paris for their fashions, working women all over the world and even the couturiers themselves kept an eye on the movies. The first of the designers to try to join movie costumes with real-life clothes was Coco Chanel, who went to Hollywood in 1929. Although her designs were elegant and innovative, by the time the movies were released, hemlines had dropped and the styles that she had created were obsolete. Nevertheless, many other designers made the pilgrimage across the Atlantic to Hollywood, including Elsa Schiaparelli, Marcel Rochas, Capt. Edward Molyneux, Alix (later Madame Grés), Jean Patou and Jeanne Lanvin. But undoubtedly the best were Hollywood's own indigenous designers such as Gilbert Adrian, Orry-Kelly and Edith Head.

Not only did women copy the dress styles of the movie stars, they also copied their hair. Created by Hollywood stylist Antoine, Claudette Colbert's bangs became a popular way of wearing hair. Also an Antoine creation was Greta Garbo's bobbed hairstyle. Women all over the world now started to copy the style by parting their hair either in the center or on the side and waving or curling their hair onto their shoulders. Another

Joan Crawford, elegantly attired, stars in the 1932 movie *Letty Linton*.

Greta Garbo stars in *Queen Christina*, 1933.

Mickey Mouse and Snow White

Walt Disney's rise to fame is a classic success story. Born in 1901, a poor boy from the Midwest, he made his way to the top with a combination of enterprise, ingenuity and hard work.

In 1928 Disney's finest creation, Mickey Mouse, made his debut in *Steamboat Willie*, the first cartoon to feature a fully synchronized soundtrack.

By the end of 1930, Mickey was an international celebrity known in Italy as ''Topolino'' and ''Miki Kuchi'' in Japan. He was such a personality that in 1931 *Time* magazine ran a feature article on him. Equally remarkable was that Walt Disney had reached a position of eminence that matched the greatest Hollywood stars and directors with only a handful of films, none of which ran for longer than eight minutes.

Influential admirers included the Italian conductor Arturo Toscanini and Russian film director Sergei Eisenstein.

Disney's first full-length animated film, *Snow White and the Seven Dwarfs*, cost close to $1.5 million to make. It was premiered at Christmas time in 1937 before a star studded audience at the Cathay Circle Theater in Hollywood. As expected, sensational reviews followed and *Snow White* went on not only to be a hit but a movie classic.

Ya Ain't Heard Nothin' Yet

Following the 1927 success of the first "all singing, all talking" movie, *The Jazz Singer*, which starred Al Jolson as the son of a Jewish cantor who embarks on a career as a music-hall singer, Hollywood soon became aware that movie audiences would no longer pay to see silent movies.

Many of the silent screen stars were unable to make the transition from silent movie acting to the more subtle styles needed for sound pictures. Actors now needed to be able to deliver their lines and act without interruption from the directors, who had previously been able to shout out their instructions on the set. Actors also needed to have good voices and clear pronounciation, which meant that many stage-trained actors rapidly replaced silent stars. Some actors ended their careers because they had strong foreign accents (like Pola Negri and Emil Jannings) or voices that somehow did not match their screen image (like Norma Talmadge and screen idol John Gilbert).

Other silent stars like Greta Garbo, Gary Cooper, Janet Gaynor and Joan Crawford were able to make the transition to sound movies with the help of voice teachers and dialogue coaches.

Sound in movies also gave rise to important new types of movies such as the musical. At first these were simply filmed versions of Broadway shows, but within a few years, thanks to the work of two men – choreographer Busby Berkley (1895–1976) and dancer-choreographer Fred Astaire (1899–1987) – the movie musical grew in sophistication to become the major type of film of the 1930s.

HEFT 20 · 1932

Vierzehntäglich 75 Pf. einschließlich 5 Pf. Bestellgeld

Mode und Heim

Ausgabe mit Versicherung

VERLAG W. VOBACH & CO. GMBH · BERLIN-LEIPZIG

variation was the long bob, created by pinning up the front and sides of the hair and leaving the back loose or curled under on the shoulder like a long page boy style.

Thanks to Hollywood, the cosmetic industry began to evolve into the giant it is today. Innovations in these years included false finger nails and eyelashes. Unlike the twenties, when makeup features in magazines had been rare, every important movie star now appeared in fan and fashion magazines and contributed to the new looks with their step-by-step guides to transforming yourself from girl next door to glamour girl – with the help of face makeup, eyeshadows, pencils, mascara, rouge and the very essential lipstick. In their efforts to look more like the Hollywood stars, women copied Marlene Dietrich's practice of plucking her eyebrows to the thinnest line. If their own eyebrows were not arched enough, they plucked them off completely and penciled in new super-thin arched brows.

Hats Off to Busby!

A successful dance director of Broadway shows, Busby Berkley went to Hollywood to work for Samuel Goldwyn in 1930, but it was not until 1933 when Berkley moved to the Warner Bros. studio that his true genius was revealed. As a dance director for movie musicals such as *42nd Street*, *Footlight Parade*, *Dames* and the *Gold Digger* films of 1933, '35, '37 and '38, Berkley developed his flamboyant visual style with the help of aerial photography, kaleidoscopic camera lenses and scores of singers and dancers.

Fashion photographers such as Cecil Beaton, Horst P. Horst, Man Ray and George Hoyningen-Heune also caught the Hollywood fever and photographed their models in a movielike style, recreating the rich tones, highlights and mood of films.

A dress in sheer black crêpe by Jean Patou of Paris, enhanced by its pale (pink) pleated sash. The diagonal pleats break out into ruffles at the left shoulder. The black hat is trimmed with pink wax flowers. A very representative late-thirties style.

"Style and Home," German style, 1932. In particular, the asymetrical collar fastening.

The Modern Woman

The new woman of the thirties was also a different shape: gone was the flat-chested, boyish look of the previous decade. Bosoms reappeared, waists were back in their normal place, and shoulders gradually began to broaden—eventually to reach the exaggerated proportions of Joan Crawford's. Curves returned as skirts were draped over hips. But the biggest fashion innovation of the decade was the backless evening gown. Popularly accredited to French couturier Madame Madeleine Vionnet, the halter-neck, bias-cut evening gowns shaped themselves to the wearer's body.

With a variety of outfits, women naturally needed a variety of shoes. In the twenties, shoe designs had been limited for the most part to "Louis-heeled" styles (resembling those worn by the French king) with pointed toes for evening wear and sturdier versions for day wear. Shoes in the thirties came in a variety of styles, heel heights and materials with pumps popular for both day (in crocodile, lizard and snakeskin) and evening (in satins, dyed to match evening gowns, brocades and silver or gold kid).

Sandals were also popular and were worn with sundresses and beach pajamas. Beach pajamas were outfits of flapping, bell-bottomed trousers plus a loose top that could be worn over a swimsuit to cover modest ladies as they journeyed from their hotel to the beach, or the cabin of their cruise liner to the sun-deck. Trousers had been worn by the more *avant garde* fashion conscious woman in the late 1920s, but they were more acceptable and more widely adopted in the thirties.

Sandals came in a variety of styles: sling back, high heeled, open-toed—and in 1936 Italian shoe designer Salvatore Ferragamo introduced the wedge heel, in which the sole and heel of the shoe were constructed

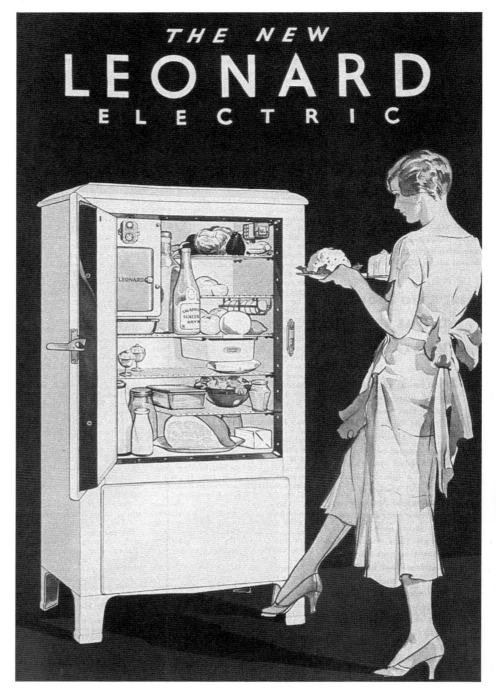

THE NEW LEONARD ELECTRIC

Labor-saving in the home: the electric refrigerator makes its appearance, allowing the housewife in the ad to cook dinner in her evening dress.

from a wedge-shaped support, without the usual space between. In 1938 Ferragamo introduced the platform sole—shoes where the height of the sole—shoes where the height of the soles had been increased to form a thick platform on which the front of the foot rested. It was even possible to produce combinations: open toed, sling-back platform wedges!

By 1939 daytime shoes had developed into practical, low heeled, broad toed shoes of rather clumpy design. It would be some years before many women would have the opportunity to wear more dainty styles.

16

Vital Accessories

While the wealthier woman might own a number of outfits suitable for many different occasions, to a vast number of women, the world of fashion clothing was unattainable. Many women simply had to make their clothes last longer and, wherever possible, they altered their clothes by adding new trimmings to hats and coats, and new collars and cuffs to dresses. Although the styles of the early thirties were more complicated to make and required more fabric than the simple short, straight-lined styles of the 1920s, resourceful home knitters and dressmakers still managed to look fashionable. Basic types of clothing, separates such as knitwear, blouses, skirts and button-up shirt-style dresses became the foundation upon which many women built a fashionable image. A change of hairstyle, a new scarf, bag or brooch helped to keep up appearances and spirits.

The large department stores catered to the modern woman's needs. Not only would she find the basic household goods, furnishings and clothing under one roof—here the fashionable woman could also buy those important little items that finished off her outfit.

Costume jewelry in semi-precious or even fake plastic stones had been popular since the twenties and, by the thirties, costume jewelry departments in stores could be extensive. Rhinestones and diamanté earrings and clip sets were popular. Most fashionable were heart-shaped or stud earrings, while the dress clips were often larger versions of the same shape. These clips were worn fastened to scarves or collars and sometimes worn as a pair on the neckline of a dress. Placed at either side of the neckline, the clips pulled the neck of a dress open and down, forming a diamond or heart-shape – the so-called sweetheart neckline.

Accessories like belts, handbags and hats were also very important parts of an outfit. Autumn and winter styles for hats were based on rather masculine shapes, with high crowns trimmed with a matching or contrasting band of ribbon. Tyrolean-looking hats with feather trims or veils were also popular. Hats with curled or shovel-fronted brims were worn tilted on the forehead, and turned up at the back to reveal neatly waved or roll-curled hairstyles. In the summer, shiny straw hats were the most popular. These were usually fairly large saucer shapes trimmed with artificial fruit or flowers and worn at an angle. Often an elastic band was attached to the inside of the crown, which was pulled over the back of the head to hold the hat in position. The elastic band was concealed under the waves and curls of the hair.

Gloves were also important, and were selected with great care to complement each outfit. With city clothes, suede or soft kid leather wrist gauntlets or elbow-length gloves would be worn. More expensive gloves had decorative features like scallopped edges and embroidered details. Less fancy short gloves in leather, wool or in combinations of the two were worn with more casual country clothes, while knitted gloves with fancy patterns and colors were popular with home knitters, younger girls and winter sports fans.

The number of outfits ultimately determined the number of accessories a woman had and so each time she changed her clothes, she changed her handbag. Small neat bags continued to be popular in the thirties with evening dresses but as the day silhouette became fuller larger bags became more fashionable. In contrast to large thin envelope bags held under one arm, very soft leather or suede was draped onto an often elaborately worked clasp to give a classical draped style to a bag, which hung from the arm on broad strap handles. For summer wear, handbags were most often made in linen or straw with appliqued or embroidered motifs to match the colors and fabrics of summer suits and dresses.

Hitler and the Nazis

Adolf Hitler was no ordinary political leader. Nor did the Nazi party conduct itself like a traditional political party. Great emphasis was placed on visual and verbal impact, by using uniforms, the swastika emblem, mass rallies and constantly repeated slogans. Political meetings were not held in small rooms but were cleverly stage-managed public events. But the message of the Nazi party was kept simple: traitors both inside and outside Germany had caused its defeat in 1918 and had since conspired to keep Germany weak. The Nazis demanded that these traitors be replaced with "loyal" Germans like themselves, so that Germany could once again be strong.

Hitler's belief was that Germany was the natural and rightful ruler of Central and Eastern Europe, but he also believed that leadership was being denied to him by an international conspiracy of Jews and communists.

Two issues obsessed Hitler: race, and what was called *Lebensraum* – the securing of an agriculturally productive living space for the German people. Convinced that when different races intermarry they become degenerate, Hitler sought to safeguard the "purity" of the Germans by adopting a policy of anti-Semitism. Persecution of Jews began soon after the Nazis came to power.

Berlin Olympics

In 1936 it was the turn of Germany and the city of Berlin to host the Olympic Games. Adolf Hitler attempted to turn the entire occasion into a spectacular display of Germanic, or Aryan, superiority and the will-to-win of the "master race."

Unfortunately for Hitler, black American athlete Jesse Owens, who won four gold medals and broke two world records, made a mockery of his racial policies. Hitler refused to present Owens with his medals, and rumors claimed that he rolled on the floor in fury.

Despite the poor showing of the Aryan athletes at the 1936 games, Hitler still commissioned German filmmaker Leni Riefenstahl to make a spectacular documentary of the events. *Olympiad/Olympic*, the result, was finally released in 1938. Although it is a testament to athletic achievement, it was also a strong propaganda piece for Hitler's Germany, one that delivered a message that good health and physical well-being were byproducts of Nazism.

America's Jesse Owens leads the field on his way to winning the gold medal in the 200-meter race, Berlin Olympic Games, 1936.

Winter Olympics, 1936. Held in Munich, to complement the summer games in Berlin later that year. Note the skier's red scarf and helmet – and also the streamlined, form-fitting ski-wear.

Body-conscious and health-conscious men and women took to physical fitness in droves in the thirties, dressed in knee-length shorts and sports shirts made of open-weave fabrics or, in Britain, in the brief, black satin shorts and sleeveless white satin blouses of the uniform of the Women's League of Health and Beauty. The ultimate fashion accessory of the thirties was a suntan, preferably for Europeans gained at one of the fashionable French resorts of Le Touquet, Cannes or Biarritz.

Throughout history, fashion had dictated that suntans were undesirable since they were associated with outdoor work and hence peasant life. Fashionable women had always tried to keep their complexions as pale as possible by covering up their skin under yards of skirts, hats and sunshades. In the late twenties Coco Chanel started the vogue for sunbathing, and it was during this time that a suntan became synonymous, not with work, but with leisure. Naturally, sunbathing produced the need for yet another fashion accessory – sunglasses, which were quickly popularized by the Hollywood stars.

DEUTSCHLAND 1936
IV·OLYMPISCHE WINTERSPIELE
GARMISCH - PARTENKIRCHEN
6:16 FEBRUAR 1936

Rising Sun

Both the American and European leaders and peoples were somewhat unclear about the trends in Europe in the thirties and were undecided about what steps to take, however, they were becoming increasingly anti-Nazi. This trend was further encouraged by Germany's association with Japan. Both countries were seen as cruel and power hungry, promoting oppressive domestic policies and external aggression. In 1936, Japan and Germany signed the Anti-Comintern Pact, in which they agreed to exchange information about international communist activities and together plan countermeasures.

In 1931, Japan's increasing need for economic recovery after the effects of the depression, its need for raw materials for industry, and the ambitions of its political and military leaders converged: Japan invaded Manchuria in China on the pretext of protecting the economic interests of the Japanese-owned South Manchurian Railway Company.

While Japanese diplomats assured foreign statesmen that the military operations were a temporary measure and that their troops would be withdrawn as soon as possible, the advance of the Japanese forces in China continued unabated. It became clear that Japan was a threat to the spheres of influence and colonies established in Asia by the European powers in earlier centuries and that war in Europe would be seen by Japan as a green light to seize these colonies.

Fashion for Everyone

Being fashionable was not of course simply confined to the ladies. Men's clothes were also heavily influenced by royalty and filmstars.

With the exception of colored sports clothes, men's clothes in the thirties were quite dull. Setting the trend for menswear in this decade was the Prince of Wales, later King Edward VIII—the man who would give up the throne of England to marry the ultra-fashionable American divorcée, Mrs. Wallis Simpson. The Prince of Wales set the trend for American-style trousers, wide-legged pants fitting snugly around the hips. For evening he revived the fashion for wearing white vests under his dinner jacket.

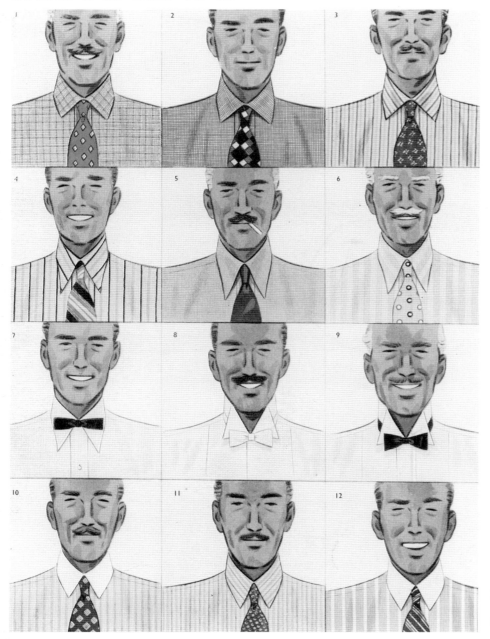

Style for men, spring 1938. Twelve different collar and tie schemes featured in *Simpson's Magazine*, a leading journal of the influential London tailoring business.

Mrs. Wallis Simpson and the duke of Windsor get married. He is formal, in standard men's morning dress. Mrs. Simpson shows her flair for fashion in a wedding dress from the American designer Mainbocher. Tell-tale details include the gathered bodice and ornamental buttons.

Coronation clothes from Jaeger. Red, white and blue capture the patriotic spirit, wide hats and nipped waists show Paris influence at work.

For men, a broader figure with wide shoulders and an athletic look was much admired. Sensing the changing mood, Hollywood film studios made fewer films featuring the romantic, sensitive heroes that had been popular with female audiences in the 1920s. Men were now portrayed in more masculine and earthy ways. Movies with war themes became popular, with the male lead playing the role of a dashing, daring pilot. The men who portrayed the gangsters in the movies may have been less good-looking than earlier stars, but they were now the tough guys, he-men and strong, silent types. Many young men in an effort to impress their sweethearts took to wearing long, loose overcoats or raincoats with the collars turned up, in a style heavily influenced by screen gangsters such as George Raft, or the emerging Humphrey Bogart.

Little Caesars

The coming of sound in the movies and the new "realism" it allowed also gave rise to a cycle of gangster movies that vividly portrayed armed violence and tough talk. Between 1930 and 1933 the brutal violence of films like *Little Caesar*, *Public Enemy* and *Scarface* provoked a public outcry.

In 1933 the Hays Office, under the supervision of Postmaster General Will Hays, intervened with the Production Code Administration, which was formed to impose certain standards on motion picture producers.

In addition to prohibiting "scenes of passion," unpunished acts of adultery or seduction, profane and vulgar language like the words *guts* and *nuts*, nudity, cruelty to animals and children or showing any representations of childbirth, the Hays Code also outlawed depictions of certain types of crime. Gangster films could no longer show machine guns or even allow the screen gangsters to talk about weapons. The code also insisted that law enforcement agents never be shown dying at the hands of criminals and that all criminal activities shown were duly punished.

In response to these restrictions, directors and producers shifted the emphasis in the gangster movies away from the gangster as a tragic hero to the gangster as a social victim. This action led to a spate of prison films like William Wylers's *Dead End* (1937), Fritz Lang's *You Only Live Once* (1937) and Michael Curtiz's *Angels with Dirty Faces* (1938).

***Little Caesar*. Edward G. Robinson tells partygoers to "reach for the sky."**

Men's clothes were very conservative compared to women's; business and social etiquette still required men to wear heavy, dark suits, collars and ties — and, of course, a hat. The most popular hat of the thirties was the trilby, a soft felt hat with an indented crown, made fashionable by Sir Anthony Eden, the British statesman. As an alternative, men could also wear fedora hats with "snap" brims that were worn with the brim up at the back and down at the front.

Many of the younger generation, especially the more Bohemian artists and writers, were very politically conscious and their beliefs were often displayed by their clothing. Since they felt that dealing with the serious world problems was more important than spending time and money on their appearances, the clothes they wore were basic and functional. Hairstyles for these young women were straight and cut off at the chin or shoulder. If it was longer it was often pinned up into a bun or worn in braids. These young men still wore their hair short but it was considered longer and less well groomed than was usual or acceptable for the thirties. Many of these men discarded their hats, which gave rise in Europe to the term "the hatless brigade," but some did wear berets as did like-minded females. Young women sometimes wore headscarves tied either under the chin or at the back of the neck, in what was considered a peasant style. For both the men and women of the hatless brigade, standard clothing consisted of basic and often leather jackets, open necked shirts or roll-neck sweaters and baggy corduroy trousers. Well polished lace up shoes were also cast aside in favor of sensible and comfortable open-toed sandals.

Children were not immune from fashion, especially well-known children. The two young British princesses Elizabeth and Margaret were followed, photographed and copied everywhere they went. In 1932, thousands of little girls in England were wearing Margaret Rose dresses, a knitted dress trimmed with rosebuds, and following a newspaper report that Princess Elizabeth's favorite colors were primrose yellow and pink, lots of little girls went to parties swathed in tiered organdy dresses of the colors worn by the future queen of England.

Style for girls. Shirley Temple stars in *Curly Top*, complete with fashionable box-pleat skirt and fitted capelet with hand-embroidered ducks. The outfit was designed by Rene Hubert, wardrobe chief for Twentieth Century-Fox.

Fred and Ginger

RKO was one of the smallest of the Hollywood film studios, but following the success of the first Fred Astaire and Ginger Rogers film, *Flying Down to Rio* (1933) – in which they weren't even given star billing – RKO became the home of the Fred Astaire–Ginger Rogers musical. Between 1934 and 1939 RKO made eight Astaire–Rogers movies, including *The Gay Divorcée* (1934), *Top Hat* (1935) and *Swing Time* (1936), which helped to make Fred and Ginger among the most popular box office attractions in America.

Although he began as a performer, Astaire went on to direct and choreograph many of his own dance sequences. Ginger Rogers, on the other hand, made her extra contribution to the movies by designing many of the lavish gowns she wore on screen.

The child idols of Hollywood were Judy Garland, Mickey Rooney and Shirley Temple – whose curls and sweetness won the hearts of millions of mothers.

There was even a product called Curly Top, which claimed to encourage children's hair to curl! Boys however would have their curls cut off and be dressed in miniature men's suits and ties as soon as they were old enough.

Fred Astaire and Ginger Rogers in action in *Top Hat*, the hit musical of 1935. Ginger Rogers wears one of her own highly distinctive designs.

Spirit of the Age

Hollywood and royalty were not the only influences on fashion design in the thirties. Designers also responded to the current trends in art, science and even engineering. One major art and literary movement of the thirties was Surrealism. The artwork featured dreamlike landscapes and strange images. The motifs used by the Surrealist artists such as Salvador Dali, René Magritte, Max Ernst, Jean Cocteau and Man Ray can be found incorporated into many designs by couturiers – especially those of Elsa Schiaparelli, who often collaborated with Surrealist artists to produce hats that looked like shoes or wicker baskets filled with butterflies, dresses with ''desk drawers'' and gloves with gold fingernails attached to them.

Style for the suburbs (1): the DeSoto "America's smartest low-price car."

The Surrealists

Surrealism was one of the 1930s' most influential art movements. It drew its subject matter from the imagination, the unconscious mind, from hallucinations, dreams, visions, fantasies and obsessions. Its leading theorist and proponent was André Breton (1896–1966), who in 1924 produced the "Surrealist Manifesto," which outlined the aims and beliefs of the movement.

Painters initially associated with the Surrealist movement were Marcel Duchamp, Max Ernst and Joan Miró. By 1930 Duchamp's place was taken by Salvador Dali and René Magritte.

Also know as Surrealists were Yves Tanguy and Giorgio di Chirico. Surrealism was also a literary movement, including such writers, as Louis Aragon, Robert Desnos, Jean Cocteau and Paul Eluard.

There was no single Surrealist style. Some paintings are eerie landscapes inhabited by objects that are not identifiable from the conscious world. Others, like Dali's "dreamscapes," place distorted familiar objects into strange locations. Magritte's paintings are more like visual puzzles: a picture of a pipe with the words "This is not a pipe," or a painting of a view through a window that turns out to be a painting of a painting of a view through a window.

Dali collaborated with fashion designer Elsa Schiaparelli on designs for fabrics and accessories, as well as Surrealist films. Meret Oppenheim, whose most famous work is a fur-covered cup and saucer, also designed earrings from champagne corks. Whatever its forms, Surrealism was a spectacularly successful movement that helped to ensure that the unconscious mind became an accepted subject for art of all kinds.

Ethiopia

In October 1935, Italy began its invasion of Ethiopia. While at first Italy's action may have appeared to be an imperialist venture in colonial expansion, the manner of the whole operation, which was marked by excessive bombing and gassing of unarmed civilians, signified something more ominous and horrifying. These actions, supported by racist propaganda, shocked other European countries. The League of Nations declared Italy an aggressor and ordered sanctions banning the sale to Italy of all essential war materials. A few countries such as Albania, Austria and Hungary refused to impose sanctions, while other countries like Germany and America agreed only to prohibit any increase in their shipments of restricted items. While the sanctions angered Italy and caused some hardships, they did not stop the war, since oil, the material most needed from other countries for the war, was not included on the sanctions list.

In secret meetings between French and British foreign ministers Pierre Laval and Sir Samuel Hoare, a settlement was devised that would allow France to keep Italy as an ally against any possible threat from Germany, by giving most of Ethiopia to Italy. The plan was leaked to the press, and public outrage at the secret deal was such that Laval fell from grace and Hoare was dismissed from office.

In May 1936 Ethiopia surrendered and a few months later, Italy celebrated the League of Nations' formal lifting of sanctions against it.

Style for the suburbs (2): Britain's Southern Railway Company became famous in the thirties for its Art Deco posters, many commissioned from leading artists. This poster contains a hidden reference to the renowned Golden Arrow – the boat-train linking London with Paris.

Smiles all round as Briton Sir Malcolm Campbell realizes he has broken the world land speed record at Daytona Beach, Florida, in 1932.

Campbell wears a zipper overall, turtleneck sweater and leather helmet with goggles – typical racing car driver garb of the time.

Spain

In 1936 a Nationalist revolt broke out in Spain led by the army. Spain's legitimately-elected left-wing government had the support of republicans, socialists, communists, anarchists, labor groups, and Catalan and Basque nationalists, all organized into a loose coalition calling themselves Loyalists. Swelling the ranks of the Loyalists were members of a volunteer force of soldiers made up of men and women from other countries who supported the republican aims. This force was known as the International Brigade and included many artists and writers. The contingent of 3,000 American volunteers was known as the Abraham Lincoln Brigade.

The Nationalists were dominated by the army, which was attempting to replace the republican government with a single-party, conservative and Catholic state. In addition to the army, the Nationalists were helped by monarchists (who supported the exiled Spanish king Alfonso XIII), a fascist "Falange," headed by Jose Antonio Primo de Rivera (the son of a former prime minister who had died in exile), and clerics who had been angered by the government's limitations to the power of the church.

Leading the Nationalist army was fascist General Francisco Franco, who had commanded army units stationed in Spain's overseas colony in Morocco. Both Italy and Germany quickly offered their support to the Nationalists, not only transporting Spanish troops, but providing thousands of their own troops, advisors, planes, tanks and ammunition. Only Russia gave any form of reliable, if limited, help to the Loyalists. Democratic governments in America and Europe chose neutrality.

In spring 1939, the Russians stopped supplying the Loyalists and the Spanish Republic finally fell after more than two years of bloodshed. More than a million Spaniards had died; thousands of refugees fled to France. But it was the bombing of the Basque town of Guernica by the German Luftwaffe that brought with it the horrifying scenes of death and destruction that made apparent to all nations the fact that warfare was no longer limited solely to opposing armies and that the modern machines of death were capable of killing civilians and even civilizations.

The 1930s were also a decade of great engineering triumphs, symbolized best in the early years by the Chrysler Building and the Empire State Building in New York City and later by San Francisco's Golden Gate Bridge in 1937. While some attempted to produce the tallest, the largest or the biggest, others competed for the honor of being the fastest. The idea of speed captured the imagination of young people in the thirties and led to fierce international competitions for all types of speed records, like the fastest transatlantic crossing by an ocean liner. World land speed records were set and broken by Briton Sir Malcolm Campbell in his car *Bluebird*, while in the air, his compatriot Amy Johnson flew her tiny Gypsy Moth *Jason* from Europe to Australia. In 1934 *Vogue* announced that the silhouettes for fashion were to have the sleek lines of a speed boat or airplane and so evening dresses fell into swallow tail points at the back, waists were pinched in, hair swept back and hats cut across the head at acute angles.

A fox-fur jacket and "bird hat" by Elsa Schiaparelli make the cover of *Vogue*, Fall 1939 – along with a streamlined locomotive train from the New York Central Railroad. Note the model's outsize "peasant" bangles.

From Munich to World War II

German expansion eastward implied the absorption of Czechoslovakia, Germany's small southeastern neighbor. The area of Czechoslovakia bordering on Germany, the Sudetenland, contained many German-speaking Czechs. The threat of imminent war waged by Hitler against Czechoslovakia led to the Munich Agreement in September 1938, giving the Sudetenland to Germany. British Prime Minister Neville Chamberlain, one of those who signed the treaty, promised that the agreement spelled "peace in our time."

The peace proved to be only a short-lived respite, during which time the major European countries continued their massive rearmament. Germany annexed the remainder of Czechoslovakia in March 1939. Negotiations between Britain, France and the Soviet Union to form a "peace bloc" against the Nazi expansion broke down when the USSR signed a non-aggression pact with Germany in August 1939. This gave the green light to further German encroachment, and on September 1, Hitler's armies invaded Poland. Two days later, Britain and France declared war on Germany, opening a war that would last until 1945 and claim some 20 million lives around the globe.

But in 1939 it was to be all change on the fashion front. As Europe became involved in World War II, fashion designers and magazines stressed economy, simplicity and practicality. For many women the clothes they had bought in 1939 were the last they would invest in for a long time. Now they had to make do and mend.

Dancing in the Depression

Gowns to Beat the Blues

Despite failing economies, many women saw it as their duty to be fashionable. As people tried to compensate for the grayness of everyday life in the depression, they turned their leisure time into something special by way of their clothes.

Evening clothes became very different from day clothes. In earlier decades, when the wealthy had set the styles, there had been no real need for them to wear practical day clothes, or to reserve the really impractical styles for evening. Now, despite the depression, all kinds of women were leading active and productive lives. They required simpler fashions for daily wear, while their luxurious long gowns were kept for evening. Evening dress for men remained formal – dinner jacket, tuxedo or tails.

In 1930 *Vogue* summed up the day and evening looks of the year. They all came from the Anglo-Danish actress Gertrude Lawrence's wardrobe for Noel Coward's play *Private Lives*, and were designed by the Paris-based American Mainbocher: fur trimmed tweeds and a bias-cut evening dress of paneled white satin.

Peelin' the Apple

Suitably attired for the evening, people could escape the bleakness of everyday life at the theater, where they were captivated by the lyrics and melodies of Jerome Kern, Cole Porter, George Gershwin and Noel Coward. But an even more popular entertainment in these years was dancing.

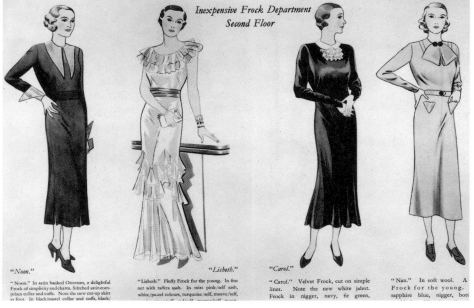

Inexpensive Frocks designed on the latest fashionable lines
Call and inspect the hundreds of chic styles in Swan & Edgar's

Inexpensive Frock Department Second Floor

"*Noon.*"

"*Noon.*" In satin backed Ottoman, a delightful Frock of simplicity and charm. Stitched satin comprises collar and cuffs. Note the new cut-up skirt at foot. In black/pastel collar and cuffs, black/

"*Lisbeth.*"

"*Lisbeth.*" Fluffy Frock for the young. In fine net with taffeta sash. In mist pink/self sash, white/pastel colours, turquoise/self, mauve/self,

"*Carol.*"

"*Carol.*" Velvet Frock, cut on simple lines. Note the new white jabot. Frock in nigger, navy, fir green,

"*Nan.*"

"*Nan.*" In soft wool. A Frock for the young. sapphire blue, nigger, bott

Inexpensive frocks for morning and afternoon, 1934.

In the twenties the popular dances were the Charleston and the Black Bottom – but in the thirties you needed rhythm and had to know how to "swing." The swing music of Americans such as Fats Waller, Jack "The Gate" Teagarden (*gate* meaning the ability to swing), Count Basie, Artie Shaw and Duke Ellington set dancefloors humming from the ritziest nightclubs and ocean liners right down to dance halls. Even in your own living room – in front of the radio – everyone and anyone Lindy-hopped, Shagged and danced the Big Apple (the forerunner of the jitterbug and whose name was a euphemism meaning "bottom"). You needed more than rhythm for steps like Kicking the Mule, Truckin' and Peelin' the Apple – these dances also required complete unself-consciousness, something that

in America was no doubt encouraged by the repeal of Prohibition in 1933 (the manufacture and sale of alcohol had been made illegal in the United States in 1920). The more restrained could still tango or take to the dance floor to the sounds of the big bands led by Henry Hall, Jack Payne, Glen Miller and Tommy and Jimmy Dorsey. Some more traditional dancers favored the fox trot and the Lambeth Walk, which originated in England in 1938.

Offshoots of commercial swing music included Latin American rhythms like the rhumba, with its hip swaying movements, that were ideal for drawing attention to the flowing lines of draped, bias-cut dresses. Lindy hoppers with their more acrobatic dances needed a different set of dancing

Summer in Town

Left: Two afternoon outfits, the first in a pale beige crêpe de chine with darker beige spots, the coat trimmed with blue fox. The second in black crêpe with white spots and green with white spots; white hat and collar

Three versions of the useful straw boater hat, showing the variations in the sizes of the crown

Right: Suit of heavy printed silk with pleated skirt and tight-waisted jacket with frills; muslin blouse

A more elegant chain-store look for 1939: tightly-belted waists, gathered sleeves, wide-brimmed hats.

Gentlemen Drivers

Another popular way of keeping the blues at bay in the thirties was by automobile driving. Those fortunate enough to own a car, whether it was a Ford "Tin Lizzie" or one of the fancier sports models, drove off to the new "roadhouses," some of which had restaurants and others, especially in Britain, had swimming pools and dance floors. For these outings the jacket-and-skirt outfit was an essential part of every chic woman's wardrobe, over which one wore one of the new 3/4-length swagger style coats with épaulettes at the shoulders, or on wetter days, a military-styled trench coat.

Gentlemen drivers ideally sported heavily greased hair, a little moustache in the manner of Hollywood star Ronald Colman, a single-breasted jacket and a pair of plus-fours – a form of knickers – worn over diamond patterned woolen stockings. The lounge lizard type of man, smooth and languid with clipped sideburns, wore cufflinks, shirt studs, tie pins and carried a cigarette holder.

Being correctly dressed for the occasion was not something that fashion alone dictated. In the thirties, social duty and status also demanded the correct hats, dresses or suits be worn. Suspenders, and certain styles of boots and caps were not acceptable. There might be a depression and war might be around the corner, but no fashionable man or woman could drop their standards.

clothes—for women, blouses and sweaters with a short flared or pleated skirt, white bobby sox and flat shoes. For their partners, the look was created by loose trousers and sweaters.

The best loved of all the dancers were also Hollywood idols—Fred Astaire and Ginger Rogers, who throughout the decade dazzled audiences with their intricate routines and left everyone humming *Cheek to Cheek*. Dancing was also a popular way to keep fit or get thin in the thirties.

Fred and Ginger kick up their heels.

A new dance, the Lindy-hop.

American tailoring: Middishade Blue custom made suits of 1931. Plus Middishade Gray and Brown.

Tailor-made clothes for spring '32, from Lucile of Paris. The dress on the left is trimmed with four brass buttons, worn over a beige "chemisette." A boldly-colored scarf contrasts with the blue-and-white diagonals of the center dress, while the beige suit at the right features a jacket falling to a point at the back. Collar and cuffs are trimmed with brown astrakhan.

Styles for Fall 1933. Subdued colors, asymetrical fastenings, three-quarter length skirts, fur trimmings, tiny clutch-bags and berets all make their presence felt.

Hooray for Hollywood!

Stars of the Silver Screen

In the midst of pre-war gloom and economic depression blazed the irresistible glamour of American films. The screen goddesses of the thirties – Joan Crawford, Greta Garbo, Jean Harlow, Marlene Dietrich or Mae West – were models whose looks and mannerisms many women tried to copy. Furthermore, the cinema also acted as a showcase for chic, avant-garde interiors: there was a preference for films in which the settings were department stores, beauty salons and glamorous homes. Shot in black and white, the Hollywood movies popularized the characteristic Art Deco style of the period.

Marlene Dietrich stars as seductive nightclub singer in *The Blue Angel* (1930). In temptress garb of rayon stockings, she fascinates and then destroys an elderly professor, played by eminent German actor Emil Jannings.

Virtue: thirties screen goddess Greta Garbo, wearing the Eugenie hat designed for the movie *Camille* (1936) by Adrian.

Certain stars were style models and the outfits they wore became important features of the film – exerting a direct influence on the fashions that were available in the stores. One of the top Hollywood designers was Gilbert Adrian (1903–1959) who had started his West Coast career creating clothes for the silent movie star Rudolph Valentino. Later, when Adrian joined the M.G.M. studios, he designed costumes for Crawford, Harlow and Norma Shearer. For Garbo, in the 1929 film *A Woman of Affairs*, he created the "slouch hat," a larger-than-normal cloche hat worn at an angle, pulled down over the forehead. It proved to be influential on hat design for the next 10 years. In 1936 Garbo again wore an Adrian creation, the Eugenie hat in the film *Camille*. Trimmed with ostrich feathers and partially obscuring one eye, the Eugenie hat was widely copied.

In 1932 Adrian designed a dress for Joan Crawford that was so popular that Macy's department store in New York reported selling over half a million dresses in similar styles. The dress in question was the Letty Lynton dress, a wide shouldered, white organdy dress with ruffled sleeves, extended shoulders and nipped in at the waist.

Although a year earlier, the influential fashion trade paper *Women's Wear Daily* had reported that French designers were exaggerating the widths of shoulders with new cuts, revers and capelets, Adrian's Letty Lynton dress accelerated the conversion to the wide-shouldered style. The optical illusion that broad shoulders created by making waists and hips appear narrower was a design device that emphasised a woman's shape. Attraction was directed down to shapely legs and ankles.

Each of the stars had their own look, created for them by their designers. Greta Garbo, for instance, was known for her page boy hairstyles, tailored suits and in particular her belted trenchcoat worn with dark glasses, a beret or a floppy brimmed hat.

The Blonde Bombshell

Blonde hair was greatly admired, much sought after and quite easily achieved. Many of the starlets in Hollywood were groomed to be blondes and platinum blonde was the ultimate in blondeness. Jean Harlow, the most famous of all the platinum blondes and sex symbols of the decade, usually appeared in her films slinking

about in satin bias-cut halter-neck gowns. In her short career, Harlow, the Blonde Bombshell, inspired thousands if not millions of women to bleach their hair, with varying degrees of success. Placed in a dish, peroxide was brushed on the hair – often with a toothbrush – and reapplied until the desired effect was achieved.

For millions in film audiences glamour meant Marlene Dietrich. Often cast as a sophisticated, somewhat mysterious femme fatale, Dietrich's clothes were dressy but not fussy, tailored but never too masculine. Despite the new skirt lengths, Dietrich somehow always managed to show off her elegant and shapely legs. While Mae West displayed her Edwardian hour-glass figure in tight fitting floor-length dresses, it was Joan Crawford who gave the second half of the decade another universal fashion: the bright red bow-tie shaped mouth.

Hollywood in Fashion

The looks and clothes of the Hollywood stars were not the only thing that women copied. The type of women the actresses portrayed were to have their effects on women's behavior, language and gestures. The restless, flightly flappers of the 1920s were now replaced by a new "modern" type of woman – glamorous, articulate and independent. The perfect match for their "tough guy" partners.

Hollywood did not restrict itself solely to glamour. It also spawned crazes for pseudo–historical fashions like small, round, open-weave Juliet caps and long velvet dresses as worn by Norma Shearer in *Romeo and Juliet* or boater hats with ribbons as worn by Katharine Hepburn in *Little Women*. None of the costumes in these films were in fact historically accurate, as the costumes were always modified to meet star approval and suit contemporary tastes.

But just when it seemed that Hollywood designers could get away with anything, the 1934 Hays Code of censorship was imposed. As well as rules that banned certain language, subjects and behavior from the screen, the Hays Code also meant that revealing dresses and dresses cut low in the front were banned. Filmmakers worked around the restrictions and devised new situations for their characters, while the designers cut away at dresses, but this time to reveal a "safe" area of women's bodies – their backs.

The impact of Hollywood was such that magazines like *Vogue* began asking whether Hollywood or Paris was creating the new fashions. In fact, it was more of a swapping of ideas. European designers Marcel Rochas, Alix, Edward Molyneux, Jean Patou and Jeanne Lanvin all traveled to California to design for films, and the film designers also made trips to Europe, researching material for their creations. Furthermore, the stars themselves with their new fortunes traveled to Europe to be dressed.

In 1935 Elsa Schiaparelli opened a boutique on Place Vendôme, a Paris shop that was the first of its kind and the model for what nearly all couturiers would do in the future. Schiaparelli's first private customer was Anita Loos, author of *Gentlemen Prefer Blondes*, and throughout the decade, Schiaparelli dressed a galaxy of stars—among them Marlene Dietrich, Claudette Colbert, Norma Shearer and Gloria Swanson. When Mae West sent Schiaparelli a life-size plaster caste of herself in the pose of the Venus de Milo as a model for the dresses she had ordered to wear in her film *Sapphire Sal*, the plaster figure inspired the shape of the bottle for Schiaparelli's perfume *Shocking*.

A dress of "feather-texture" for Joan Crawford.

Blonde bombshell. Jean Harlow in 1933. Halter neck, bias-cut silk and exaggerated fur trimmings underscore her sex appeal.

Follow the Yellow Brick Road. Judy Garland stars in technicolor in *The Wizard of Oz*, a story of escape from the world of the depression to the colorful, magical dreamland of Oz.

The King of Hollywood: Clark Gable.

Art Deco: Themes and Machines

Streamline Style

Art Deco was a style that drew on the art of many different cultures for its motifs. In the 1920s the elements of the style had been taken from African and Pre-Columbian art and, after the discovery in 1922 of Tuthankamen's tomb, Egyptian themes became highly popular alongside motifs of fountains, gazelles, hunting dogs and zebras. In clothes, these elements were incorporated into fabric designs and pieces of jewelry.

By the 1930s, the hallmark of the Art Deco style was its geometry, which was largely derived from the Cubist movement. Motifs, which included everything from flowers and animals to the human figure, became angular, but the subjects that were most popular were the hard-edged forms of zigzags, electric flashes and sun ray motifs.

A further important aspect of the Art Deco style was streamlining. For many people speed was one of the marvels of the modern age, and the shapes and lines that functioned effectively in aerodynamics became incorporated into many designers' work. The geometric shapes of Art Deco lent themselves perfectly to strong colors and contrasts with red, black, white and silver being one of the most popular and fashionable color combinations for all types of design.

The best examples of the Art Deco style are to be found in the sky-scraper. Skyscrapers grew from the problems of constructing buildings in restricted spaces such as in Chicago and New York. But skyscrapers also became potent symbols of commercial power, and many were built in

The folds of this evening gown by Alix are finely complemented by the flowing drapery of the "winged victory" sculpture.

towns and cities where building space was not in particularly short supply.

Manhattan Skyline

The most famous of all the sky-scrapers built in the 1930s are in New York City. Begun in 1931, Rockefeller Center is a complex of offices, shops, restaurants and theaters that included the RKO Roxy movie theater and Radio City Music Hall. The Empire State Building of 1931 rises 102 stories above the city and, at the very top, a mooring for airships was provided. Unfortunately, the updrafts and currents created by neighboring tall buildings made using airships in cities impossible.

The best example of the Art Deco skyscraper is the 1930 Chrysler Building. Its overall shape is a ziggurat, or stepped pyramid, topped by a tower and spire with sculpted decorations. The decorations were inspired by automobile parts like radiator grilles and hub caps. Not only does the building suggest the wealth of the Chrysler Corporation, but in its decoration, the building may also suggest the Chrysler car.

The greatest stylistic innovation of the depression era was streamlining. In America the style was encouraged by a wave of European designers who came to the United States to escape the fascism that was on the rise in Europe and the imminent war. But the prophet of streamlining was industrial designer Norman Bel Geddes. Many of Bel Geddes's ideas were visionary rather than practical, but through his efforts streamlining became the accepted style, a style that also came to be seen as a symbol of optimism and promise for the future, since the style suggested a nation moving forward out of the depression to become the powerhouse of the new machine age.

Lee Lawrie's 45-foot-high statue of Atlas sets the Art Deco tone for New York's Rockefeller Center, begun in 1931.

Material Advances

The nature of the streamlined style made it suitable for almost every purpose. Not only were the headquarters and factories of the manufacturing giants built in the style but so were small gas stations, bars, restaurants and movie houses. The materials these buildings used were modern and inexpensive: enamels, plastics, wood, and aluminium could all be produced in pre-fabricated units. The streamlined style represented everything that was forward-looking, modern, clean and efficient.

The styles and materials of streamlining proved themselves to be flexible enough for use not only on the super-sleek transcontinental trains and skyscrapers but for a wide range of low-cost, mass-produced consumer items like kitchen appliances, radios and even fashion accessories.

The belief that something inexpensive could also be fashionable first appears with the Art Deco style. In earlier decades, fashion had been more or less confined to the wealthy, who were happy to pay for expensive materials and exclusive designs. One designer who captured the new spirit was Gabrielle (Coco) Chanel. In addition to a range of clothes with simple lines in inexpensive fabrics such as cotton, Chanel's designs could easily be copied by the home dressmaker. Chanel also helped to popularize costume jewelery made of inexpensive materials liked plastic. Plastic was chic simply because it was a novelty, but was cheap enough to be available to everyone and versatile enough to mimic ivory, ebony, jade or coral. Fashion could now be mass-produced and the make-believe glamour of the movies could belong to everyone.

Silver-blue lamé gives a
machine-metallic finish to this
dramatic evening design.

38

A blue-and-white striped suit of 1936
shows many Art Deco influences in
the pattern, cut and detailing.

Streamlining (2): the Phantom
Corsair, designed by Rust Heinz. A
1937 styling exercise for the "car of
the future," it looks some 20 years
ahead of its time.

Traveling clothes of 1932 from
Woman's Journal. The short red
jacket in heavyweight cloth suggests
the freedom needed for driving, as
well as more passive modes of
travel.

New Materials: Revealing the Body Beautiful

From Silk to Rayon

Not only did the clothes that women wore in the 1930s become more womanly – women also wore fewer of them. The new curvy shape that women sought was helped along by a variety of fabrics, some old and some new, that could be cut and draped to show off the wearer's body.

In addition to the various silks, wools and linens that had always been used for fashionable clothing, designers now had at their disposal a range of synthetic materials. Since these new fabrics could be produced inexpensively, they were often used for mass-produced items of clothing. There were some designers, however, notably Elsa Schiaparelli and Victor Steibel, who would incorporate synthetic materials into their haute-couture range.

Since the late 19th century, the search for synthetic substitutes for natural materials had concentrated on silk. Silk was the most expensive raw material for cloth because it was the hardest to produce. The mulberry tree from which the silkworms feed will grow only in certain climates. Experiments in the last years of the century led to the development of artificial silk, later called rayon, which was made of wood cellulose treated with chemicals to produce long silk-like threads. The new fiber, when woven into cloth, not only produced a fabric that draped well, but one that also had a high absorbency, allowing it to be dyed successfully.

Since it looked and felt like silk, rayon could be used for lingerie at the less expensive end of the market, and since it was also washable, a whole range of ready-to-wear, crease-resist-ant dresses in all colors – from the palest pastels to the deepest blues – became available.

Rayon was also widely used for stockings but in 1939 it would be replaced by a new fabric, nylon. Nylon was the result of a research program started in 1927 by Dr. Wallace H. Caruthers at the Du Pont Company in Delaware. In 1938, Du Pont produced nylon commercially and in the following year successfully tested it in knitted hosiery. By the end of the decade, nylon stockings had replaced the often shiny and poorly fitting rayon ones.

Rayon and nylon are perhaps the two most familiar synthetic fabrics from a whole host of intriguingly named materials. Cellophane is also familiar to us, but we do not usually associate it with fashion, yet it was out of this material that Alix created an evening dress that was likened to the wing case of a shiny black beetle. Victor Steibel used cellophane in conjunction with a white taffeta accordian-pleated gown in 1936 that was modeled in *Vogue* by Vivien Leigh.

Artificial crêpe is the material for this cinema frock – a new material for a new kind of social occasion.

Delightful Cinema Frock. *New Afternoon Frock*

"lory." Crêpe Carioca, a lovely new terial is used for this smart Frock. Note

"Gilda." Delightful Cinema Frock in dull artificial crêpe. Designed with new and

"Gwen." Delightful Frock made of wool with angora finish. Note the very smart

"Gilleta." Smart Military Cl Dress, suitable for town or st

Fabrics Galore

Metallic fabrics were also popular: lamé is the name given to fabrics woven with flat metallic threads. It was immensely popular for evening wear. Sequins and beads made from colored plastics and glass also helped to swathe women's bodies in shimmering effects of light.

A less well known fabric, Rhodophane, had been developed in the 1920s by the French company Colcombet. Rhodophane was a mixture of cellophane and other synthetic fabrics that created a glass-like fabric that was versatile enough to look like clear glass or have a gauzy, cobweb look. Despite its fragile appearance, Rhodophane was used by Schiaparelli for a range of dresses and accessories, including handbags and even shoes.

New synthetic materials were not just confined to evening wear and lingerie. Accessories and leisurewear also received a boost from these new fabrics. Elastic yarns made of rubber combined with silk, cotton or rayon produced a fabric ideal for swimwear, since it clung to the body and didn't lose its shape when wet. Plastic materials were also important, since they could be molded and colored to create jewelry, handbag frames, belt buckles and sunglasses. Plastic zippers in matching or contrasting colors were pioneered by Schiaparelli, first in sportswear and later in evening dresses.

Artificial fabrics give a new freedom to the lingerie and leisurewear designer.

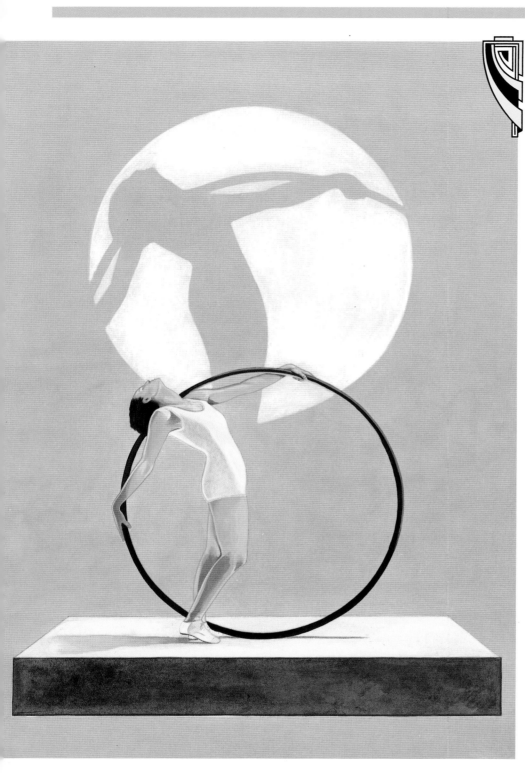

Cult of the body beautiful. The hoop used as a prop here symbolizes the ever-expanding culture of physical fitness, and its new linkage with fashion and glamour.

Beachwear styles of 1935 in Krepe-Tex from the American Charnaux company, promising fit "as never before."

Top tennis star Bunny Austin takes advantage of the freedom the new designs in men's shorts offered sportsmen.

White rayon suit from Dorville, 1938. The Surrealists seem to have taken over this particular fashion shoot.

Halter Necks and Bias Cuts

Madame Vionnet Cuts It

In the 1920s, a well-known couturier called Madame Madeleine Vionnet had devised a method of cutting fabric called bias cutting. This involved cutting across the grain of the fabric and had two distinct advantages over ordinary cutting techniques, despite the fact that it required a greater width of material. First, when a dress was made up of bias-cut pieces, the fabric draped in sinuous folds and, where it touched the wearer's body, it clung to it. Second, the dress would stretch sufficiently to allow the wearer to put on her dress over her head or by simply stepping into it – without the need for any additional side, back or front openings.

By using the bias-cutting techniques, designers could produce gowns in silk, satin, chiffon and crêpe that would cling around the bosom, waist and hips and flare out from the thighs into an elegant sweep of skirt. The bias-cutting technique continued in the thirties, but the evening dresses now had an added new element: they were backless. Some dresses would be held up by narrow shoulder-straps, while others had halter-necks, where the high panel of the front was tied around the back of the neck, leaving the back and shoulders completely exposed.

Hollywood's Back Plunge

It has been argued that the fashion for plunging backs came from Hollywood, where the stricter film censorship codes prevented actresses being shown in dresses cut low at the front. Filmmakers tried to get around this by cutting away at the backs of dresses. It was also likely that the bare-backed style was influenced by the increasing fashion for sunbathing and swimwear designs, which were cut low at the back to maximize the area of tanned skin.

Whatever its origins, the new fashion for evening dresses was certainly elegant. In order to attract even more attention to backs, there was a vogue for wearing strings of beads or pearls swinging down at the back and artificial flowers pinned at the base of the spine. Elsa Schiaparelli even went as far as to design a backless dress with a bustle that jutted out like a shelf.

A flowing georgette evening gown of 1930, with full scarf and trimmed skirt. A single string of pearls hang from the back of the model's neck.

Paris designs for winter 1935: low backs, bias cuts, diagonal seams.

Satins and Furs

To complement the sweep of the skirt, many women carried large, brightly colored chiffon handkerchiefs. Also popular for evening wear were fox furs. Entire animals, or better still two animals, were draped over bare shoulders. The most sought after furs were those of the silver fox, but ultra-fashionable women wore white fox capes for evening.

For day wear, bias-cut skirts that flared from the hips lent themselves to a new fashion for stripes and checks on the bias, but for evening, heavy crêpes and dull satins gave flowing, folding and draping dresses their most statuesque qualities. The greatest draper and molder of jersey, silk and wool was Alix Barton (later known as Madame Grès), who opened her own fashion house in Paris in 1934. With great patience and skill Alix pleated fabrics into precise shapes that while they were elegant and simple, they also resembled Greek sculptures.

Tunic and skirt by British couturier Captain Edward Molyneux, 1936. The back-flared tunic almost recalls the bustle of the late 19th century.

A classic design. The designer is Alix (Madam Grés), the date 1937.

"The interest begins at the top!" A selection of evening gowns from 1932. Of particular interest are the varying treatments of sleeves and shoulder straps. Waist down, things are a little more standardized.

Designs from 1936 by Lucien Lelong (left) and Jean Patou (right). The Lelong design twists mulberry and emerald ribbons into a column that extends down the spine; Patou slashes the front of the predominantly black dress to introduce a rainbow of colors beneath.

A classic backless evening design from Madeleine Vionnet.

Schiaparelli and the Surrealists

Objects and Illusions

One of the major international art movements of the thirties was Surrealism. Initiated in the 1920s by André Breton and drawing on the Dada movement, dreams and Freudian analysis, Surrealism was initially concerned with the written and spoken word. Later, the Surrealists became fascinated by objects. To the Surrealists, "objects" were exercises in "displacement": removing an object from its usual setting and placing it somewhere else caused a disruption in its traditional role, scale and association.

Familiar objects set in unusual locations or settings not only shocked the viewer but insisted that the spectator made new interpretations of the scene.

Influential on art and literature, Surrealism also began to affect fashion. And not only in the way that fashion was presented – in illustration, photography and window displays. The clothes themselves were affected too.

Mutton Chops and Slippers

The designer most influenced by Surrealism was Elsa Schiaparelli. Born in Rome in 1890, her friendship with Dada and Surrealist artists such as Francis Picabia, Man Ray, Marcel Duchamp and Tristam Tzara dated from the 1920s in Paris. Schiaparelli's first commercially successful design was for a "trompe l'oeil," (fool the eye) sweater: a simple black wool sweater but with a simulation of a white butterfly bow at the neck. The sweater proved an instant success and enabled Schiaparelli to establish a business in Paris, that concentrated on sportswear, tailored clothes and evening wear. But Schiaparelli liked nothing better than to amuse – either through wit or shock tactics – and like her Surrealist friends she was also fond of displacing elements – using tweed for evening clothes and burlap for day dresses. Her interest in unusual fabric led her to design with synthetic materials like cellophane or Rhodophane and the French company of Calcombet in Lyons also supplied her with a fabric printed with newspaper clippings – clippings about herself, naturally!

The classic exercise in Surrealist fashion displacement was the Shoe Hat, product of a collaboration between Schiaparelli and Surrealist artist Salvador Dali. As early as 1932, Dali had posed for a photograph wearing his wife Gala's slipper on his head, and in 1937 he designed the now famous Shoe Hat for Schiaparelli. In a true Surrealist cycle of events, Dali then photographed Gala wearing the Shoe Hat dressed in a suit with lips for pockets. Other Dali–Schiaparelli creations included the Ice-Cream Cone Hat and the Mutton-Chop Hat, which went perfectly with a suit embroidered with cutlet motifs.

Fabric designs by Christian Berard and Jean Cocteau were complemented by a range of accessories: clear plastic necklaces decorated with colored metal insects that appear to crawl directly on the wearer's neck; handbags that look like bird cages; ceramic vegetables and aspirins as necklaces (designed in conjunction with poet Louis Aragon) and glowing brooches and buttons shaped like paperweights or grasshoppers.

Also imaginative and inventive was Schiaparelli's use of zippers, which she incorporated into the designs of garments. A simple dress with a zipper in a contrasting color may not seem outrageous now but at the time it was completely new.

A Shocking Experience

Surrealist notions also extended to Schiaparelli's perfumes. She had two fragrances devised in the thirties: Shocking and Sleeping – Schiaparelli had a preference for names beginning with her own initial. The bottle for Shocking was designed by Surrealist artist Leonor Fini, who created an hour-glass shaped bottle based on the silhouette of Hollywood actress Mae West. The bottle for Sleeping took the form of a candlestick – a reference to the world of dreams, always a potent source of Surrealist imagery.

Although Schiaparelli had been "shocking" her clients throughout the decade, her true moment of triumph came in the 1937–1938 season. Returning to trompe l'oeil effects she produced a jacket inspired by Jean Cocteau embroidered with clasped hands at the waist, with the profile of a woman's head of hair, suggested by gold bugle-beading, flowing down one sleeve. With Dali's help she also created the Lobster Dress: a giant, pink cooked lobster surrounded by sprigs of parsley printed on to an organdy dress.

The Harlequin collection produced the domino motif that was a hat. The Circus collection showed the words "Beware of Fresh Paint" on the back of a dress, as well as a Chicken-in-a-Basket, Quill-Pen and Ink-Well hats. As

Surrealist artists played games with people's expectations about art, Schiaparelli transformed the greatest of all the illusionistic devices, clothing, by letting the unexpected take the place of convention.

Dali also helped design the fabric for Schiaparelli's Tear Dress and matching cape. An evening gown designed to be worn at the most formal of functions, it gives the illusion of having been torn repeatedly. The cape did in fact have real tears in it, so the outfit – even when brand new – appeared to have already been destroyed.

Elsa Schiaparelli, 1938. The famous Tear Dress, with matching cape.

The bird provides the chief Surrealist
diversion in this otherwise fairly
orthodox Schiaparelli evening gown.

Shocking, Schiaparelli's perfume
"from the heart of France."

The famous Fingernail Gloves,
teamed with a three-quarter length
black evening dress.

Schiaparelli creations in wool for
daytime wear, 1938. The fabrics are
jersey and tweed, the pinched waists
are beltless.

A Schiaparelli evening coat in tweed,
1936. The reverse is lavishly beaded
for contrast, the headdress shows
Asian influences.

Shaping Up: Health and Fitness

Sport for All

During the thirties, physical activity and sun-worshipping assumed cult proportions. One of the manifestations was the Women's League of Health and Beauty, founded in Britain by Prunella Stack in 1930. In their uniform of brief, black satin shorts and sleeveless white satin blouses, thousands of league members gave public demonstrations of physical fitness, based on the principle that a trained body was the secret to a simple but happy life.

All over England and Continental Europe naturist clubs, health and sports societies were formed to pay homage to the body beautiful. Nudism and hiking had come from Germany and all through the thirties Austria and Germany were fashionable European holiday destinations. The effect on fashion was a trend toward Tyrolean peasant dirndl skirts, shorts and feathered hats as youngsters and adults joined hiking clubs.

People were so involved with keeping fit that a strike by French taxi drivers in 1936 began a craze for bicycling.

Naturally, special cycling shorts-suits were a must!

Even if you didn't take part in any sporting activity but were content to watch, the fashion-conscious woman could wear what the fashion magazines called spectator-sports clothes. In the spring and autumn these were skirt-suits and coats in tweeds and checked wools, while in summer, navy blue jackets and white skirts were considered appropriate wear for watching tennis or polo matches.

The navy blue and white combination was also popular wear on cruise ships or at holiday resorts. To emphasize a nautical look, motifs such as anchors and ship's wheels were embroidered on pockets and lapels.

Freedom of Movement

With the increased popularity of active sports, designers of sportswear now had to address the functional needs of the sports (rather than simply altering existing day-wear styles), while at the same time maintain a fashionable silhouette. Active sportswear had to allow for maximum movement. Skating skirts were now shorter than they had ever been, well above the knee and pleated or flared for movement and an eye-catching line. The sport itself was given a boost by the champion skater-turned-Hollywood-star Sonja Henie, who skated her way through her films in a variety of lavish one-piece skating dresses.

Elastic tops for tennis pants and shorts – goodbye to suspenders! These chainstore styles for men and women date from 1934.

MOTORING AND SPORTS WEAR.

MAN-TAILORED COSTUME.
Obtainable in a variety of the newest styles and materials. To order. From £7 7 0

FOR MOTORING.
In natural Chamois, with Sleeves.
£2 12 6

LEATHER AND SUEDE SPORTS JACKET.
In fine quality.
Colours: Brown or Tan shades.
From £3 13 6

TWEED SKIRTS.
To order 63/-

A PRACTICAL MOTOR COAT.
Made of Semi-chrome Leather and lined Tweed.
Obtainable in chocolate or tan shades.
From £3 13 6

SLEEVELESS CHAMOIS LEATHER WAISTCOAT.
For Hunting or Sports wear.
£1 7 6

Motoring and sportswear for women, 1938. Suede, leather and tweed predominate, neckties and scarves are popular. Cuts echo the forms of evening wear, though in more robust materials.

Winter sports grew in popularity and a skiing vacation became an annual event for those who could afford it. Fashionable ski outfits in the thirties consisted of matching jackets and trousers that were worn tucked into lace-up ski boots and finished off with a weatherproof cap.

Fun in the Sun

As the "fun-in-the-sun" mentality encouraged a heightened sense of body-consciousness, men's and women's sportswear became more and more revealing.

Standard tennis wear for men had long been long white flannel pants, with the cuffs turned up for play, white shirts with rolled-up sleeves, white socks and white, crêpe-soled shoes. Fashion conscious players in the thirties started to opt for one of the French tennis star René Lacoste's short-sleeved shirts, with a small collar, buttons and the famous crocodile (known as an alligator in the U.S.) emblem on the chest. Some amateur players, finding the long flannels too hot and uncomfortable, switched to shorts. But professional players still played in long pants until 1932 when Bunny Austin took the plunge into shorts at the Men's National Tennis Championships at Forest Hills, New York.

Bare legs for women on the tennis courts was a trend started in 1928 by the Spanish player Lili de Alvarez, who competed in a just-below-the-knee culotte dress designed by Schiaparelli. Total freedom of movement came in 1933 when Alice Marble wore shorts at the Wimbledon championships.

Bare on the Beach

Designers were also cutting away at swimwear. In the 1920s men had worn one-piece swimsuits that covered their chests. Gentlemen who bared their chests in public were not only considered disrespectful but also risked being arrested. By 1932 men at private beach resorts began to follow the European lead of swimming without shirts. Helped by the craze for suntans, which became an international cult in the 1930s, the most popular swimsuits for men and women were those that offered maximum body exposure. Once men had cast off their shirts, they then began to alter the trunks: legs were cut higher and new knitted fabrics like Lastex promised a figure-hugging fit. A variety of styles offered men solutions to the problems posed by the laws governing decency on public beaches: the Jantzen Topper model of 1934 had a zipper waist that allowed for the attachment of a swim-shirt when decorum ruled. By 1935 attitudes had changed sufficiently to allow men at most public beaches to swim in trunks alone.

Women bathers, in their pursuit of greater freedom and maximum exposure, eventually abandoned the yards of over-skirts and shirts of the earlier swimwear styles and adopted a one or two-piece swimsuit based on the male prototype.

Yachting outfit in elasticated fabrics, topped with a rubber bathing cap.

Ai Signori piace lo "Jantzen,,

AI SIGNORI PIACE LO STILE BUONO .... se pratico e combinato col conforto. Lo *Jantzen* piace perché ad un aspetto elegante unisce la massima libertà nel nuotare. Lavorato a maglie strette con lana fortissima di fibra lunga. lo *Jantzen* si adatta al vostro corpo perfettamente, *senza una piega!* Data la sua straordinaria elasticità lo *Jantzen* mantiene sempre la sua forma elegante.

Sono illustrati il *"Twosome,,* e il *"Speed-Suit,,*. Li troverete senza bottoni o con bottoni infragibili di gomma. Come tutti i *Jantzen* sono lavorati a maglie strette con lana fortissima di fibra lunga. Esaminate i modelli a vivaci colori per Signori, Signore e fanciulli nei principali negozi. Colori resistenti perché già tinti nel filato. Il vostro peso indica la misura del costume. Badate alla marca di fabbrica "Bagnante rossa che si tuffa,,, che ogni vero *Jantzen* deve portare.

Chiedete al vostro fornitore Il prospetto con la tavola dei colori armonizzanti o scrivete direttamente all' ITALO AMERICAN TRADING COMPANY, VIA LUIGI CALAMATTA 16, ROMA (126).

Jantzen

Il costume che vi dà libertà nel nuotare
MADE IN AMERICA

Swimming costumes for men, from the renowned Jantzen label. Stretch fabrics made possible these novel designs.

The athletic male body beautiful. Poses such as these show the cult of physical prowess at its height.

Panty-girdles in Lastex from the Kestos Company of America. Under bias-cut satin, such skin-tight underwear was a must.

Weekend casual wear from France, 1939. The military influence in fabrics and cuts is unmistakable.

The End of the Rainbow

The Gathering Storm

By 1936 the worst years of the depression were over and the number of unemployed people began to decrease. It was also the year that the political sky grew darker. Adolf Hitler in Germany and Benito Mussolini in Italy were drawing closer together. In July, the Spanish Civil War broke out. It was seen by many as the showdown between the political left and right in Europe and was claimed on both sides to be the greatest crusade of modern times.

Spain had legally elected a left-wing government against which General Francisco Franco had rebelled. In spite of the legitimacy of the Spanish government, 28 other governments adopted a policy of non-intervention. By the spring of 1937 there were 80,000 Italian and 30,000 German troops in Spain fighting on the side of Franco. Although many Europeans and Americans were concerned about events in Spain, and some joined the International Brigade and fought on the Republican side against Franco, there was little they could do to affect the events and outcome of the war.

When the German Condor Legion air force bombed the Basque town of Guernica and practically wiped out the entire population, the world was outraged. Pablo Picasso's famous painting *Guernica* commemorating the event went on tour throughout

End of the line: two typical suits of 1938, with broader shoulders and boxy jackets. A foretaste of the military styles of the war years. Hats and button details, however, show these designs to be rooted firmly in the pre-war era.

Europe in an effort to raise people's consciousness about the war. But it seemed clear that in the end the victory would go to Franco. Greatly encouraged by their exploits in Spain, Hitler and Mussolini (now the Berlin–Rome Axis) began a gigantic buildup of their own forces.

War was not only confined to Europe. In the same year, Japan invaded China, seizing Beijing and Shanghai and forcing the government to move to Hankow and uniting Chiang Kai-shek with the Chinese communist forces led by Mao Zedong and Zhou Enlai. It was only a matter of time before the storm broke over the world.

Gearing Up

In these troubled years, fashion designers responded to and reflected the prevailing mood. Daytime fashion looks became more severe and militarily-inspired, with square-épauletted shoulders, frog closings, feathered hats, gauntlet gloves and sensible low-heeled shoes. Like soldiers, women were expected to be meticulously groomed and to pay attention to every tiny detail.

By 1938 it seemed obvious that war was not far off. That season's designs were seen by *Vogue* as being useful "factory" looks. Hair was pinned up safely and hidden under headscarves, suits were broader shouldered and skirts were a little more skimpy using less fabric. In contrast, however, evening dresses cast a nostalgic look back at a more romantic and peaceful past with crinolines (stiff underskirts), tight waists and frills.

A year later Europe was engulfed by war, but not before a whole new industry of ready-to-wear clothing manufacture had been established catering to the needs and desires of people who wanted moderately priced, fashionable clothes. As thousands of Europeans fled the oppressive regimes in their homelands to seek refuge in Britain and America,

Styles for men going on vacation, not to war, February 1939.

many skilled tailors, seamstresses and dressmakers became available in the manufacturing industries – bringing not only their labor, but a sense of Continental style, which had been lacking in some areas of British and American design.

In 1939, the European couturiers went to war with clothes that were practical and in most cases, the last they would design until peace was restored. Shirt-waist dresses and simple suits were designed not to date; sweaters and trousers became acceptable fashion wear. Makeup artists like Helena Rubenstein and Cyclax responded with spiritedly named lipsticks such as Regimental Red and Auxilli-

ary Red. Schiaparelli produced designs in Maginot Line Blue and Foreign Legion Red before embarking on a lecture tour of the USA, where she would spend most of the war years.

There was one trend that emerged very briefly in 1939, only to disappear. Closely defined waists began to appear in the Paris collections. In contrast to her earlier styles, Coco Chanel showed tight-waisted, full-skirted dresses while Mainbocher displayed full-skirted dirndls. Not until Christian Dior's New Look in 1947, the first postwar fashion to have a strong impact, would slim waists be featured again so strongly. For the time being at least, there were to be no more escapist follies or fashion fantasies. All over the world practical fashions were in style.

Travel style for men, 1938. Heavy tweed coats over pinstripe suits – a mixture of formality and comfort. Scarves provide a splash of color.

Tailored linen suit from Maggy Rouf, which looks forward to styles and cuts of the following decade. The flower-decked Suzy hat claims inspiration from French Impressionist painter Claude Monet.

Color makes a comeback; outdoor outfits by Margaret Barry, Eva Lutyens and W. W. Reville-Terry.

One more surreal creation from Schiaparelli.

Glossary

Adrian [Gilbert Adrian] (1903–59) American designer of stage costumes for Broadway shows until 1925, when he moved to Hollywood to make clothes for Rudolph Valentino. After working with Cecile B. De Mille, Adrian moved to M.G.M., where he designed costumes for Greta Garbo, Joan Crawford, Jean Harlow and Norma Shearer. In addition to trend-setting hats like the Eugenie, Adrian is also credited with the creation of the wide-shouldered style of dresses as worn by Joan Crawford. His most famous creation of this type was the Letty Lynton dress in 1932, a white organdy dress with ruffled sleeves and a narrow waist.

Alix (Madame Alix Grès) (1910–) French designer, whose original intention had been to become a sculptor. Grès began her career by making *toiles* – muslin couture designs – that she sold to other fashion houses. In 1934 she opened her first fashion house as Alix Barton, where she became renowned for her ability to drape and mold silks and jerseys until they resembled the flutes of classical columns. Often using asymmetric shapes, bias cuts and dolman sleeves in her designs, Grès's work achieved a simplicity and elegance that is unmatched.

Antoine (1884–1976) Hairstylist. Polish-born hairdresser Antoine gained his experience in the salons in the fashionable European resorts of Biarritz, Cannes, Deauville and Nice, as well as in Paris and London. From 1925 to 1939 Antoine commuted between Paris and New York, where he ran a beauty practice in Saks Fifth Avenue. As well as being credited with the popular Shingle Cut of the late 1920s, Antoine also designed the upswept hairstyles of the thirties and was responsible for the creation of Greta Garbo's long bob and Claudette Colbert's bangs. A popular Antoine style was a blonde or white lock on an otherwise dark head of hair.

Art Deco A style of architecture and design originating at the Paris Exposition des arts decoratifs (1925) and continuing through the 1930s. Art Deco concentrates on heavy, simplified geometric forms.

Bias Cut A method of cutting fabric across the grain, devised in the late twenties by Madame Madeleine Vionnet. Panels of fabric cut on the bias and stitched together gave dresses the ability to cling in certain areas, like the bust and hips, but also to create long sweeping skirts that flared out from the thighs. Since this method of cuttings and construction allowed the fabric to be stretched, dresses could be stepped into or placed on over the head without requiring any extra openings.

Chanel, Gabrielle ("Coco") (1883–1971) French designer, who began working under her own name in 1914. In 1930 Chanel went to Hollywood to design for several films made by the United Artists company. In 1931 she showed a range of evening dresses designed to promote cotton as a fashion fabric. Much of her attention in the mid-thirties was focused on manufacturing. In 1939 she closed her salon in Paris. In 1954, at the age of 71, Chanel reopened her salon.

Cocteau, Jean (1889–1963) French artist, stage designer, illustrator, poet and playwright. Closely associated with the fashion world through his links with the theater and his friendship with Elsa Schiaparelli, with whom he collaborated on designs for accessories. As an illustrator, Cocteau also designed covers for a number of fashion magazines, notably *Harper's Bazaar*.

Dali, Salvador (1907–1987) Spanish-born painter and Surrealist famous for his dreamlike landscapes and such images as melting watches. In addition to designing fabrics for Schiaparelli, Dali also contributed many ideas to jewelry and fashion design.

Dirndl Originally a peasant garment, thought to have originated in the Austrian Tyrol, dirndls have full skirts, loosely gathered onto a waistband that falls in soft pleats. In the thirties, the widespread pastimes of walking and hiking made dirndl skirts popular wear.

Ferragamo, Salvatore (1898–1960) Italian shoe designer. At the age of 16 Ferragamo joined his brothers in California where he made shoes by hand for the American film company,

Universal Studios, Warner Bros. and M.G.M., as well as for private clients. Returning in 1927 to Italy, in 1936 he set up a workshop in Florence to be the first large-scale producer of hand-made shoes. In 1938, Ferragamo was credited as having originated the wedge heel and platform sole. He also experimented with materials like cork, lace, raffia, shells and nylon. By 1957 Ferragamo had created over 20,000 styles and registered some 350 patents.

Halter-neck Created by the high panel of the front of a dress or blouse being tied around the neck, leaving the back and shoulders exposed. The halter neck is credited to Madame Madeleine Vionnet and was popular for evening wear and beach clothes in the 1930s.

Head, Edith (1899–1981) American costume designer and head designer at Hollywood's Paramount studios from 1938 to 1967. With over a thousand film credits, Head designed for Marlene Dietrich, Mae West and Dorothy Lamour, for whom she designed a sarong in 1936 (for the film *Jungle Princess*) that was widely copied as beach-wear.

Lacoste, René (1905–) French tennis star nicknamed "le Crocodile" because of his aggressive style of play. On his retirement from professional play in 1933, Lacoste launched a white, short sleeved tennis shirt that had a small collar, buttons at the neck and the small crocodile emblem on the chest. (Although in the U.S. they were called alligator shirts.) Popular leisurewear for men since the thirties, Lacoste shirts now come in a variety of colors.

Lastex Trade name of the American Rubber Company's elastic yarn made of rubber combined with silk, cotton or rayon and used for lingerie and swimwear.

Mainbocher (1891–1976) American-born designer. He started his fashion career with *Harper's Bazaar* as a fashion artist. Later he became fashion editor, then editor-in-chief of French *Vogue*, where he remained until 1929. In 1930, Mainbocher became the first American to open a successful couture salon in Paris, where he was famous for his evening wear. International publicity followed when he created a wedding gown for Mrs. Wallis Simpson for her marriage to the duke of Windsor and created a vogue for Wallis Blue. Like Chanel, his last Paris collection in 1939 previewed the New Look of 1947, with small waists and tightly laced corset-like bodices. In 1939, Mainbocher returned to the U.S. where he opened a salon in New York, which remained open until 1971.

Plus-fours Knickers made of tweed or worsted and originally favored by golfers, plus-fours were popular menswear in the thirties, particularly for those favoring automobile driving as a pasttime.

Rayon The name given to an artificial silk made of cellulose fibers. Rayon draped well and could also be dyed. In 1912 the first rayon stockings were made. In 1916, knitted rayon became popular, soon followed by outerwear made of the material. Since it looked and felt like silk, rayon was a popular substitute for silk in the production of less expensive lingerie.

Rhodophane A mixture of cellophane and other synthetic fibers, developed by Colcombet of France with a glass-like appearance. Rhodophane was used by Schiaparelli to produce dresses, handbags and shoes.

Schiaparelli, Elsa
(1890–1973) Italian-born designer. After spending her early married life in Boston and New York, in 1920 Schiaparelli moved to Paris. One of her first designs was for a trompe l'oeil (fool the eye) sweater – a black sweater with an illusionistic white bow at the neck. In 1929 she opened her own salon specializing in evening wear, tailored clothes and sportswear. She often collaborated with leading artists like Salvador Dali and Jean Cocteau, and many of her designs were inspired by Surrealism. As well as using unconventional materials for her clothes, Schiaparelli also used plastic zippers in contrasting colors, placing them in exposed places, thereby making their use both functional and decorative. Her designs included hats in the form of ice-cream cones, lamb chops and shoes. She also launched a range of fragrances and cosmetics.

Steibel, Victor (1907–1976) South African-born designer. While studying at Cambridge in England, Steibel designed costumes and scenery for the Footlights Revue in London. In 1929 he became an apprentice at the London couture house of Reville and Rossiter, which specialized in formal gowns for clients of the royalty and aristocracy. In 1932 Steibel opened his own house and, in addition to producing bias-cut evening gowns, he also produced romantic dresses for stage and screen actresses. Experiments in synthetic fabrics led to the creation in 1936 of a taffeta and cellophane gown for Hollywood film star Vivien Leigh.

Surrealism An art movement started in the 1920s and founded by André Breton. The leading artists of the movement were Salvador Dali, René Magritte, Man Ray, Max Ernst, Francis Picabia, and Jean Cocteau. Writers involved included Paul Eluard and Louis Aragon. Surrealism concentrated on fantasy by recreating dreams and the subconscious in art forms.

Vionnet, Madeleine (Madame)
(1876–1975) French-born designer. One of the most innovative designers of her day, Vionnet is credited with the introduction of the bias-cutting technique, the popularization of the halter neck and cowl neck. Vionnet conceived her designs on miniature models, draping fabrics into sinuous folds with which she rose to fame throughout the twenties and thirties.

Reading List

A great deal has been written and published about the 1930s – this reading list is only a very small selection. Magazines and movies of the period are another excellent source of information.

Adult General Reference Sources

Calasibetta, Charlotte, *Essential Terms of Fashion: A Collection of Definitions* (Fairchild, 1985).

Calasibetta, Charlotte, *Fairchild's Dictionary of Fashion,* 2nd Edition (Fairchild, 1988).

Gold, Annalee, *90 Years of Fashion* (Fairchild, 1990).

O'Hara, Georgina, *The Encyclopedia of Fashion* (Harry N. Abrams, 1986).

Trahey, Jane (Ed.), *100 Years of the American Female from Harper's Bazaar* (Random House, 1967).

Young Adult Sources

Ruby, Jennifer, *The Nineteen Twenties & Nineteen Thirties*, "Costume in Context" series (David & Charles, 1988).

Wilcox, R. Turner, *Five Centuries of American Costume* (Scribner's, 1963).

Acknowledgments

The Author and Publishers would like to thank the following for permission to reproduce illustrations: B.T. Batsford for pages 28, 29, 36, 40, 44, 45, 49, 53 and 56; The Hulton Picture Co. for pages 8–9, 18–19, 21, 23a, 26b and 52; The Kobal Collection for pages 12, 13, 23b, 32, 34a and 35a; The Mary Evans Picture Library for pages 6, 7, 10, 14, 22, 31b, 31c, 39c, 42, 43, 46, 47, 51, 54, 55, 59 and 63; Library of Congress for page 27 plus front cover; The National Film Archive for pages 20 and 24; Popperfoto for page 37; Retrograph for the frontispiece and pages 11, 19 and 26a; The Vintage Magazine Co. for pages 16, 31a, 39b, 50 and 57. The illustrations were researched by David Pratt.

Time Chart

	NEWS	EVENTS	FASHIONS
30	107 Nazis win in German elections	Amy Johnson flies solo to Australia Youth Hostels Association formed Chrysler Building, in NYC, completed; 1046 feet high	Women's League of Health and Beauty formed in Britain
31	Japanese invade Manchuria Proclamation of Republic in Spain	Empire State Building, in NYC, completed; 1250 feet high	Chanel shows collection of 35 cotton evening dresses Mainbocher is first American designer to open a Paris salon
32	Roosevelt elected president of United States Great Hunger March of Unemployed to London	Campbell drives racing car *Bluebird* at 235 mph George Washington Bridge over the Hudson River, opened	Schiaparelli introduces a bustle to her backless evening gowns Margaret Rose dresses made popular for children by Princess Margaret in England Adrian designs Letty Lynton dress for Joan Crawford movie
33	Hitler becomes Reich Chancellor Roosevelt announces New Deal Prohibition repealed Reichstag fire	Polyethylene first made Garbo stars in *Grand Hotel*; Mae West in *She Done Him Wrong*	René Lacoste introduces short-sleeved tennis shirt Influence of Hollywood at its highest
34	Night of the Long Knives Nazi purge in Germany The Japanese make Henry Pu-yi, last emperor of China, puppet ruler of Manchukuo (Manchuria)	Ocean liner *Queen Mary* launched Duke of Kent marries Princess Marina Popular song: *Smoke Gets in Your Eyes*	Molyneux designs trousseau for Princess Marina Tyrolean look popular Alix (Madame Grès) opens Paris salon
35	Germany repudiates military provisions of Versailles Treaty Nuremberg laws outlaw Jews in Germany Mussolini invades Ethiopia	Silver Jubilee of George V and Queen Mary Radar invented Mickey Mouse appears in color	Schiaparelli opens her boutique in Paris Popular color in Britain is *Jubilee Blue*
36	Death of King George V Abdication of Edward VIII Rebellion begins in Spanish Army Spanish Civil War Rome-Berlin Axis proclaimed by Mussolini	Olympic Games in Berlin Exhibition of Surrealist art in London. Dali attends wearing deep-sea diving suit Margaret Mitchell publishes best-selling novel *Gone with the Wind*	Steibel creates Cellophane and taffeta dress Schiaparelli designs clothes and accessories in Rhodophane Surrealist influence on fashion design and illustration at its height
37	German airforce bombs Basque town of Guernica, Spain Rioting in Czech Sudetenlan Japanese seize Shanghai and Peking	First full-length Disney cartoon: *Snow White and the Seven Dwarfs* Picasso paints *Guernica* Golden gate Bridge, San Francisco completed Duke of Windsor marries Wallis Simpson	Schiaparelli launches fragrance *Shocking* in Mae West inspired bottle Italian shoe designer Ferragamo introduces the wedge heel Dali and Schiaparelli produce the Shoe-Hat
38	Nazi' Germany annexes Austria Chamberlain meets Hitler at Munich	Chaplin's *Modern Times* is released George Biro makes first practical ball point pen	Schiaparelli launches fragrance *Sleeping* Ferragamo develops the platform soled shoe
39	Germany invades Czechoslovakia Italy invades Albania Britain, Franch, Australia and New Zealand declare war on Germany Russia invades Poland and Finland	Vivien Leigh and Clark Gable star in *Gone with the Wind* German battleship *Bismarck* launched John Steinbeck publishes *The Grapes of Wrath*	Sweaters and trousers appear in *Vogue* Paris shows tight waisted dresses, a prelude to the post-war New Look Schiaparelli and Mainbocher leave Paris for the US

Anticipating the shape of the Dior "New Look", Mainbocher's collection of 1939 pointed the way to the look of the next Decade.

Index

Figures in *italics* refer to illustrations.